DINOBIBI

NEW ZEALAND

TRAVEL FOR KIDS

CONTENTS

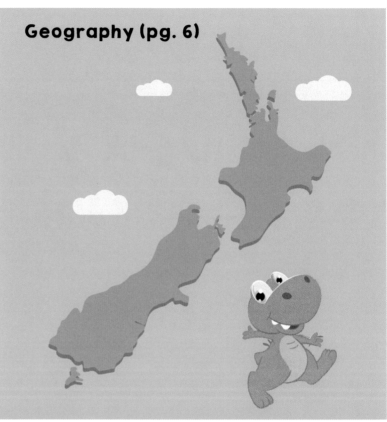

Culture and Tradition (pg. 28)

Native Plants and Animals (pg. 38)

Famous People (pg. 45)

Major Cities and Attractions (pg. 50)

Hello friends!
I am thrilled to welcome you to my stunning country, New Zealand (NZ). My name is Jack, and I am an 11-year-old boy living in Wellington, the capital of this country, with my parents. I will take you on an exciting trip across the length and breadth of my country and tell you all about New Zealand and my life here. But before that, please do tell me about yourself:

Your name:

Which country are you from:

What made you choose New Zealand for your vacation this time?

What are the places you want to visit while here?

The school education system in my country is divided into three stages:

1. Early childhood education – from birth until we enter primary school; but, this education is not compulsory, or required, for us.

2. Primary and secondary school – From 5 – 19 years of age

3. Further of higher education – Vocational education for a career

The United Nations ranks my country's school education system as one of the best in the world. Now, that is something to be proud of.

As you will have realized by now, I attend primary school (a public school) in my neighborhood, which is completely free because the government takes care of all expenses.

One last thing I have to tell you about schools in my country is that educational institutions can hold up to 1 pound of uranium for the purpose of conducting lab experiments. However, if the uranium were to explode, then the school will be fined NZD1 million.

On that interesting note, let us move on and continue with our New Zealand trip.

New Zealand, located in in the southwest Pacific Ocean, is an island country consisting of two main islands (and multiple other offshore smaller isles). The names of the two primary islands are North Island and South Island.

New Zealand is about 2000 km (1200 miles) southeast of Australia and is separated from the island continent by the Tasman Sea.

Actually, New Zealand is so close to Antarctica that expeditions to this remote part of the earth start off from here.

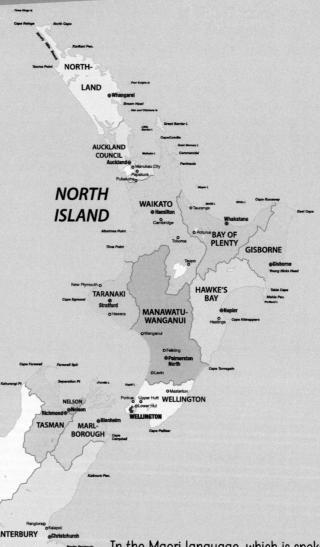

In the Maori language, which is spoken by the indigenous people of New Zealand, North Island is called Te-Ika-a-Maui, and the South Island is called Te Wai Pounamu. The Maori name for New Zealand is Aotearoa which translates to 'the land of the long, white cloud.'

In addition to these main islands, New Zealand is made up of numerous small islands scattered on the Pacific Ocean.

Pop Quiz!

Name the strait that divides the North and South Islands of New Zealand?

1. The Cook Strait
2. The Strait of Gibraltar
3. The Tasman Strait

(Answer – 1. The Cook Strait; a strait is a narrow stretch of water connected two large water bodies)

What are New Zealanders commonly called across the globe?

1. The Ostriches
2. The Kiwis
3. The Pandas

(Answer – 2. The Kiwis)

About 23 million years ago, volcanic eruptions under the ocean resulted in the formation of New Zealand. Even today, New Zealand is home to over 50 volcanoes many of which are still active.

The oldest rocks in my country are believed to be 500 million years old, which was part of the unbroken land mass when all the land on Earth was fused together as one. New Zealand sits on two tectonic plates- the Australian and the Pacific.

These tectonic plates under the surface of the earth are continuously shifting resulting in plenty of geological action, which, in turn, results in an abundance of relaxing hot springs in New Zealand, especially in the North Island.

My country has a coastline of over 15,000 km (9320 miles). The geographical landscape of this country is beautiful and stunning consisting of rocky shores, green and vast pastures, and tall snowy peaks. These landscapes have attracted many filmmakers to my country to shoot movies.

Pop Quiz!

Can you guess which of the following three movies were shot in New Zealand?

1. The Harry Potter Series
2. Captain America, the First Avenger
3. The Lord of the Rings trilogy

(Answer – 3. The Lord of the Rings trilogy)

New Zealand is long and narrow extending to about 1600 km (990 miles) in length, and at the widest part, it is 400 km (250 miles) in width.

Largely a mountainous country, it has more than 18 peaks, which are over 3000 meters (9800 feet) in height.

Canterbury Plains, Akaroa, Canterbury Region New Zealand

The South Island

The largest island of this country is the South Island with nearly 1/4th of the population residing here. The majestic Southern Alps, running for nearly 483 km (300 miles), cut lengthwise along the center of the island.

The eastern coast of the Southern Alps has the majestic Canterbury Plains and the farmlands of Southland and Otago. The western coast is famous for its rough, rocky coastline with some parts of the northern part of the South Island are home to sandy beaches.

Additionally, the western coast of the South Island is dotted with dense native bush areas and is also the home to Fox and Franz Josef Glaciers.

The North Island

The North Island has mountain ranges running right through the center with farmlands on both sides. The Volcanic Plateau, which is a highly active volcanic region, lies in the central part of the North Island.

The northern part and nearly all the eastern part of North Island have sandy beaches that are great for surfing, swimming, and sunbathing.

Rivers and Lakes of New Zealand

New Zealand has more than 3800 lakes with Lake Taupo, located in the middle of the North Island, being the largest lake in New Zealand.

My country has more than 70 major river systems covering the North and South Islands. Rivers in New Zealand were earlier used for transportation of goods.

Let me tell you some interesting things about some of the important rivers and lakes of New Zealand.

Today, most of the rivers are only used for commercial purposes, specifically for tourism and recreational activities such as canoeing, rafting, kayaking, etc.

The concept of bungy jumping, jumping off a tall structure while wearing an elastic cord, was invented by a New Zealander, and today, you can find multiple bungy jumping spots over numerous river-based scenic locales.

Lake Wakatipu – In the earlier days, Lake Wakatipu, which is the longest lake (80 km or 50 miles long) in New Zealand was used as an important means of transportation. Today, it is famous for its stunning vistas and beauty.

This stupendous lake is also the primary source of water for the people of Queenstown, which is situated on its the banks. The one drawback about this lake is that flooding is a common occurrence because five rivers feed this huge lake.

An unusual element seen in Lake Wakatipu is the formation of 'tides.' Actually, the correct word is seiche or 'standing waves' that form in a fully or partially enclosed body of water. This seiche formation results in the rise and fall of the water level in Lake Wakatipu, which happens about every half an hour.

The Maoris connect this geographical phenomenon to a legend in which they believe that this rise and fall of the water level in the lake is the heartbeat of a monster, Matau, who is sleeping in the lakebed.

You can cruise across this splendid lake and enjoy the beauty of nature. Other important lakes in New Zealand are Lake Takepo, Emerald Lakes, Champagne Pool, and Lake Wanaka.

River Waikato – Translating to 'flowing river,' Waikato is the longest river in New Zealand. The Waikato River starts off as numerous streams on Mount Ruapehu, all of which flow into Lake Taupo. This part of the Waikato River is called Tongariro River.

The river leaves Lake Taupo as Waikato River and flows through the North Island for a distance of 425 km (264 miles) before emptying into the Tasman Sea.

Visitors can participate in numerous activities on this beautiful, meandering river including boating, fishing, kayaking, canoeing, jet skiing, whitewater rafting, and riverside walking.

River Waikato flows through eight hydroelectric dams making it one of the most important power suppliers for the country.

River Whanganui — River Whanganui begins its flow from Mount Tongariro in the North Island, passes through the Whanganui National Park, and finally empties into the Tasman Sea.

The local Maori people used this river for food, transport, a spiritual home, and even as a playground. Maori settlements are found all along the banks of River Whanganui.

The Maoris caught this river's abundant eels with weirs, or traps. Slowly, these weirs were removed to make place for steamboats and, moreover, with water being channelized for hydroelectric power, the number of eels also declined.

A special walk, called Te Araroa, extends along the entire length of the river and is one of New Zealand's Great Walks. You can explore this river and its banks in multiple ways including by foot, cycle, bike, jet boat, canoe, or drive on a vehicle.

Pop Quiz!

What is the nickname of River Whanganui?

1. The Rhine of New Zealand
2. The Nile of New Zealand
3. The Mississippi of New Zealand

(Answer — 1. The Rhine of New Zealand)

River Grey — *Rising from Lake Christabel, River Grey is on the northwestern part of the South Island. This 75-mile long river is called Māwheranui by the Maoris.*
Other important rivers in New Zealand include Taramakau, Rakaia, Waitaki, Haast, Clutha, and Waiau.

River Buller — River Buller, known as Kawatiri to the Maori people, is the largest river on the west coast of the South Island. Kawatiri translates to 'deep and swift' in the Maori language.

Starting as River Travers on the St. Arnaud range, Buller flows through Lakes Rotoroa and Rotoiti, and continues its journey westward until it empties into the Tasman Sea.

The gorges of River Buller offer some of the most beautiful scenic spots for travelers. In fact, the gorge at Inangahua Junction is one of the most visited and popular tourist spots in New Zealand.

Lake Taupo

Located right at the center of the North Island, Lake Taupo sits on the crater of a volcano called Oruanui that erupted more than 26000 years ago.

This freshwater lake is a popular fishing spot for both visitors and the locals. Rainbow trout and brown trout are found in abundance in this lake.

Other fun activities you can see in this place are skydiving, waterskiing, kayaking, and canoeing.
The Maori name of Lake Taupo is Taupo-Nui-a-Tia, which literally translates to 'the great cloak of Tia.'

Pop Quiz!

Can you recall how many lakes are there in New Zealand? I have mentioned this earlier.

1. More than 1000 lakes
2. More than 500 lakes
3. More than 3800 lakes

(Answer — 3. More than 3800 lakes)

Mountains of New Zealand

Pop Quiz!

Which is the tallest peak in New Zealand?

1. Mount Cook
2. Mount Taranaki
3. Mount Tasman

(Answer — 1. Mount Tasman, it stands 3700 meters (12000 feet) tall)

Mount Cook is known as Aoraki by the Maori people. In fact, the official name of this peak is Aoraki Mount Cook.

Tasman Glacier

The Southern Alps range of the South Island has a lot of glaciers; the largest one is the Tasman Glacier, and the most famous ones are the Franz Josef and Fox Glaciers. All three glaciers are accessible through trekking or helicopters.

Nearly 1/5th of North Island and about 2/3rd the South Island in New Zealand are mountains. These mountain ranges extend from the north of the North Island right up to the south of the South Island. The silt and alluvial deposits (which make the soil rich and fertile) accumulated from the erosions of these mountains over millions of years has resulted in the vast and highly fertile Canterbury Plains in the South Island and smaller fertile plains in the North Island.

Some of the most productive farmlands of New Zealand are located in these fertile plains formed over millions of years.

Another unique feature of the New Zealand Mountains is the appearance of what are known as 'sunken mountains.' Fiordland and Marlborough Sounds in the South Island are examples of these kinds of 'sunken mountains,' which is a result of subduction, or slow submerging, of tectonic plates deep into the earth's crust.

Flag of New Zealand

The Union Jack, which is the national flag of the United Kingdom, represents the fact that New Zealand was a British colony for some time. However, this was not the first flag of the country. It was only adopted as the official flag of NZ in 1902.

Before that, the Union Jack was considered the national flag of New Zealand. However, even the Union Jack was not the first flag of my country. The first 'national flag of New Zealand' was the 'Flag of the United Tribes' before the British took complete control of the territory.

Today, the flag of New Zealand is a royal blue rectangle with the Union Jack on the top left corner and four white-bordered red stars on the right.

Other National Symbols of New Zealand

National bird — Kiwi is the national bird and the unofficial symbol of New Zealand. You can read up more about them under the Native Plant and Animal section.

By the way, the kiwi fruit is not native to New Zealand. It was brought from China just about a century ago.

Pop Quiz!

Do you know which country is the only other country that has two national anthems?

1. Denmark
2. The UK
3. The US

(Answer — 1. Denmark)

National anthem

New Zealand is a unique country which has two national anthems namely 'God Defend New Zealand' and 'God Save the Queen.'

'God Defend New Zealand' was first performed publicly in 1876 and was officially adopted as an additional official anthem in 1940 along with the existing 'God Save the Queen.'

Currency of New Zealand

There are five denominations of NZD bank notes including $5, $10, $20, $50 and $100. The coins in my country come in five different denominations; 10 cents, 20 cents, 50 cents, NZD1, and NZD2.

Given below are the approximate costs of some common everyday items.

The currency of my country is the New Zealand Dollar, which is represented as NZD.

1 dozen eggs — NZD7

1 pair of jeans — NZD110

1 liter of milk — NZD2.12

1 loaf of bread — NZD2

Languages in New Zealand

There are three official languages in my country namely English, Maori, and _____ (Sign language/Creole/Portuguese).

(Answer – Sign Language)

15

CHAPTER 2

WEATHER IN NEW ZEALAND

You can witness four different seasons in New Zealand, and each of them possesses something unique and beautiful.

Because we are below the equator, our seasons are backwards from those above the equator. Let me give you a brief idea about all the four seasons in New Zealand.

Spring in New Zealand

Springtime in my country lasts from September to November. Average temperatures during the day are around 19-degrees Celsius (66 Fahrenheit). Typically, in spring, you can expect to see swift changes of climates from sunny, crisp days to cool, and even, frosty days with some spring showers.

Lupines on the shore of Lake Tekapo New Zealand

The waterfalls in New Zealand during springtime come alive. Most visitors to our country at this time never miss out the Lord of the Rings tour, which covers spectacular gardens and valleys that break into full bloom.

Springtime is perfect for outdoor activities with multiple walks and cycle tours organized by the tourism industry. Another common sight you will get to see during spring in New Zealand is newborn lambs frolicking through the vast, green fields and pastures.

There are blossom festivals organized at Hastings in Hawke's Bay and Alexandra in Otago. Also, river rafting is best done during spring as the snow begins to melt down which increases the water levels in the rivers creating added excitement for rafters.

Summer in New Zealand

The summer months in New Zealand are from December to February. For us locals, this period is holiday time as everyone extends their Christmas holidays to visit scenic beaches and lakes.

Average temperatures in summer range between 21-degrees Celsius to 25-degree Celsius (70-77 degrees Fahrenheit) making my country warm, but comfortable. Daylight hours are long and sunny while nights are mild during summer with little or no rain nearly in all places.

Summer days are best for the beach picnics, snorkeling, kayaking, swimming, and even sailing. The Pohutukawa trees, which are native to New Zealand, bloom in summer creating a burst of beautiful, vibrant red.

Summer is also the time to learn and master surfing skills with places like Taranaki, Raglan, and Mount Maunganui known as surfing meccas of New Zealand.

You can also swim with dolphins, take coastal walking trails, and enjoy yummy seafood. New Zealand provides plenty to do during the summer months.

Autumn in New Zealand

The autumn months in New Zealand last from March to May. Autumn is only slightly different from summer with regard to temperatures and daylight hours. By mid-April, the nights get chilly.

The best part about traveling through New Zealand in autumn is that crowds are far less as compared to the summer months.

Autumn comes alive in my country, especially in the Central Otago and Hawke's Bay regions, as the deciduous trees take on beautiful colors of yellow, gold, and orange. The sky during autumn looks vibrantly blue.

Autumn is a great time to soak in the beauty of nature in New Zealand at these two places, as they are famous for their splendor.

As the days are still long, outdoor activities are great even in autumn, especially for taking one of the nine Great Walks that New Zealand is famous for. In March and April, the days are hot enough to lure you for a swim in the oceans and beaches.

Winter in New Zealand

Winter months in New Zealand last from June to August, and during this time, the mountains in the country come alive with snowboarders and skiers. You can cycle or walk on the mountain trails or take a dip and soak in one of the gorgeous hot springs.

In North Island, there is almost no winter even though the weather gets cooler than in the other seasons and there is rainfall. Average temperatures range between 10-degrees Celsius to 16-degrees Celsius (50-60 degrees Fahrenheit).

In South Island, heavy snowfall and frosty days are common. The ski season is best experienced in South Island. The mountains of Central Otago, Central Plateau, and Canterbury are covered in fresh snow on all winter days. You can try your skiing skills at various ski fields in Wanaka and Queenstown.

Sunshine in New Zealand

During the summer months, days can last until 9:30 pm. Also, there is very little air pollution in my country as compared to many other nations. Therefore, the UV rays from the sun are very powerfully felt here, especially between September and April. Protecting yourself from the harmful effects of these UV rays is very important, so use sunscreen frequently on your skin and wear sunglasses and hats.

Rainfall in New Zealand

Rainfall is very high in my country and is more or less evenly spread out right through the year. In the northern and central regions of New Zealand, there is more rainfall in winter than summer and the reverse is what happens in the southern parts of the country.
Heavy rainfall is a blessing for New Zealand because not only does it make forests thick, green, and stunning but also helps the farming, horticulture, and agriculture industries to thrive.

Snow in New Zealand

Most of the snow in New Zealand falls in the mountains including the Southern Alps in South Island and Central Plateau in North Island. Some interior parts of Otago and Canterbury also get some amount of snow in winter.

The Legend of New Zealand

As per Maori legend, New Zealand was fished out from the sea by a powerful and brave demigod called Maui. He was an extraordinary man born to supernatural parents and gifted with outstanding warrior skills.

He was so strong and brave that he was able to trap the sun and also tame fire. But, his biggest achievement was to fish out the North Island. Here is how Maui accomplished this amazing feat.

Maui had four brothers who were all jealous of his skills and strength. One day, they decided to leave him behind at home and go fishing. However, Maui overheard their plans.

He used an ancient jawbone to carve out a magical fishhook, then he quietly crept under the floorboards of his brothers' canoe and hid there. The brothers went far out into the sea before Maui revealed himself.

He threw his magical fishhook into the sea and chanted some powerful incantations, or divine prayers,. The hook continued its downward journey into the ocean until Maui felt it hit something very deep below. With the help of his four brothers, he pulled up the hook bringing a gigantic fish to the surface.

Maui told his brothers to wait until he finished his prayers to appease the god of the sea, Tangaroa. But, they got tired and started cutting up the fish. And that is how valleys, mountains, coastlines, lakes, and rivers were formed.

Now, I told you the Maori names of North and South Island earlier. Let me tell you that again with the meaning.

North Island is called Māori as Te Ika a Māui which means 'Maui's fish,' and South Island is called Te Waka a Māui which translates to 'Maui's canoe.' Isn't that a great story? Now, on to some historical information about my country.

Early History of New Zealand

The first people to arrive in New Zealand were the ancestors of the present-day Maoris. Historians believe that immigrants to New Zealand might have come from other islands in Polynesia between 1200 and 1300 A.D.

These early Polynesian were seafarers and explorers, and they might have discovered New Zealand on one of their exploration trips across the Pacific Ocean. These early Polynesian settlers developed the Maori culture.

The statue of Kupe, on the Wellington waterfront, shows the legendary explorer with his wife, Hine Te Aparangi, and his tohunga (priest), Pekahourangi

Even today, the Maoris believe the Kupe was the first explorer to discover New Zealand. This great sailor used the guiding power of stars and various ocean currents to help him navigate across the Pacific.

Kupe left his homeland, Hawaiki, in Polynesia and ventured on his traveling adventures. People believe this man made landfall at the Hokianga Harbor in the North Island about 1000 years ago.

Although the island of Hawaiki is not visible on the modern map, the Maoris believe their first New Zealand ancestor came from a group of islands called Polynesia in the South Pacific Ocean.

Even today, there are many similarities between Maori and Polynesian cultures and languages practiced in Tahiti, Hawaii, and the Cook Islands. After Kupe, more sailors from other islands came and landed at different points on the coast of New Zealand.

Hunter-Gatherers and Growers

The early Maori people were expert hunter-gatherers and fishermen too. They used flax fiber to weave fishing nets and stones and bones to carve fishhooks.

Traditional maori storehouse

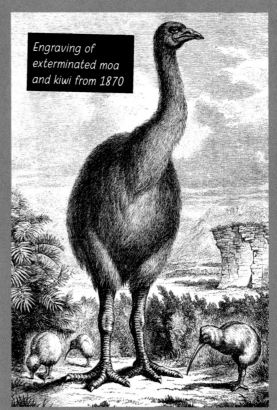

Engraving of exterminated moa and kiwi from 1870

They expertly hunted native birds and animals of New Zealand including moa, the largest bird in the world, which is now extinct. The moa birds grew up to 12 feet in height and weighed up to 230 kilograms (507 pounds)! If these settlers had been able to hunt and kill such huge creatures, they must have made highly creative and innovative traps and nets.

These early Maori settlers also cultivated land and grew vegetables like sweet potato, or kumara, which they brought from their native Polynesian islands. They also ate locally available native fruits, vegetables, berries, and roots.

They built storehouses, or pataka, on stilts to store their food and keep it safe from raiding animals.

The Maori tribes were always fighting with each other. The men were strong and powerful and were skilled warriors who could use a variety of weapons like taiaha, or spear, and mere, or club. Even today, these traditional weapons are used in Maori festivals and ceremonies.

Each tribe built a strong fort or fence around their village, or iwi, to protect from attacks from other tribes and intruders. Such fortified villages are referred to as 'pa' in the Maori language. Even today, you can find historic pa sites all across the country.

Maori warriors with tattoos, celebrating Waitangi Day,

Europeans in New Zealand

The first European to discover New Zealand was Abel Tasman in 1642. He called the newly discovered island Staten Landt and made it part of the Dutch country.

He first made contact with the Maoris at the Golden Bay in the north of the South Island. Abel Tasman wanted to start a friendly relationship with the Maoris who were coming towards his ship in two canoes. Unfortunately, some misunderstanding took place, and a small battle happened here in which a few Dutch sailors died.

After this incident, Abel Tasman did not set foot on New Zealand and returned home with a report that nothing of importance was found here.

In 1769, the British rediscovered New Zealand when Captain James Cook went to Tahiti to observe and record certain planetary movements in the sky. This British sailor sailed around New Zealand two times and mapped it successfully.

The early New Zealand settlers from Europe were mostly missionaries, whalers, and sealers. Whalers and sealers are people who hunt whales and seals. These early Europeans and Maoris had great trade relationships.

But, the Maori population declined for two important reasons namely:

- Guns were provided by the Europeans for inter-tribal wars.
- The diseases brought by Europeans killed many Maoris.

The Treaty of Waitangi

By 1840, the population of Maori was around 125,000 and that of the settlers was 2000. After 1840, in addition to missionaries, whalers, and sealers, merchants and traders also started arriving in New Zealand.

These merchants traded timber and flax with the Maoris for guns, clothing, and other such items. However, not all merchants provided a fair deal to the locals.

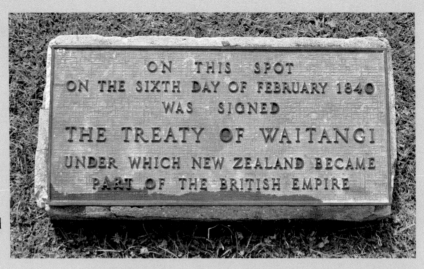

ON THIS SPOT
ON THE SIXTH DAY OF FEBRUARY 1840
WAS SIGNED
THE TREATY OF WAITANGI
UNDER WHICH NEW ZEALAND BECAME
PART OF THE BRITISH EMPIRE

Numerous Maori chiefs approached William VI, the King of England then, for protection from unfair trade practices from dishonest traders and to keep their territories safe from French invaders.

As the population of British settlers increased, the government decided to reach a peaceful agreement with the Maoris to set up a British colony in New Zealand, which resulted in the Treaty of Waitangi which was signed in February 1840.

This historic treaty between the British Government and 43 Maori chiefs from North Island was signed at Waitangi on February 6, 1840. After that day, the treaty was taken all across New Zealand, and more than 500 Maori chiefs also signed it.

However, by 1860, conflicts broke out between the Maoris, especially in North Island, and the British, which came to be known as the New Zealand Land Wars. The British emerged victorious, and very soon, most of the land was owned by the settlers.

This important treaty is considered as the country's 'founding document.' The building and the place in which the Treaty of Waitangi was signed is still preserved as the Waitangi Historic Reserve which is a popular tourist attraction.

Economic Growth and Development

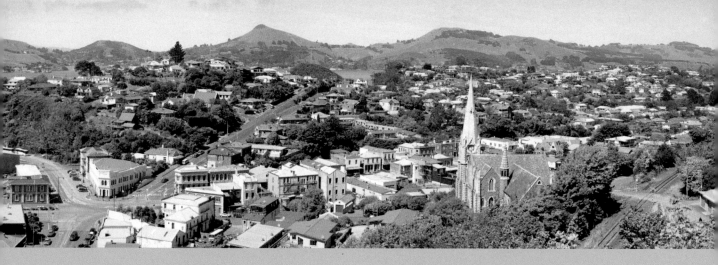

While the land wars in the country left the North Island in conflict, the South Island prospered during this time. Sheep farming was set up on vast grasslands in the South Island with Canterbury becoming one of the most prosperous provinces in the country.

Gold was discovered in 1861 in Otago first, and then on the West Coast of South Island which resulted in Dunedin becoming the largest town in the country.

The export business in New Zealand started in 1862 when the first batch of frozen meat was shipped successfully to England. Soon, New Zealand became one of the largest suppliers of meat, cheese, and butter to Britain.

With agriculture growing rapidly, forests were cut down to make place for farmlands and cattle ranches.

Socially and financially, the country grew in leaps and bounds. New Zealand was the first country in the world to give voting rights to women way back in 1893. New Zealand is also the first nation to set up housing plans and pensions for workers.

Modern-Day New Zealand

Right through the 19th and 20th century, British culture had a big influence on New Zealand's culture and transformation into a modern country. All education, administrative, and cultural measures and policies were based on British models.

New Zealand soldiers participated in all the wars that the UK fought in including the Boer War, World War I, and World War II as part of the British army.

We are truly proud to be KIWIS!

After the end of World War II, although New Zealand's ties with the British remained strong, it also made new friends. New Zealand signed and entered into the ANZUS Pact in which ANZUS stands for Australia, New Zealand, and the United States. New Zealand soldiers helped the US by participating in the Vietnam and Korean Wars.

Despite a powerful colonial influence, the country of New Zealand has a unique identity of its own today that combines British and Maori influences. It has its own trading and foreign policies and maintains its sovereignty with pride and nationalistic fervor.

Provinces of New Zealand

Presently, there are 16 provinces, or regions, in New Zealand, and each of them is governed by a local government. The names of the 16 political areas are:

1. Wellington
2. Auckland
3. Northland
4. Nelson
5. Otago
6. Southland
7. Taranaki
8. South Canterbury
9. Hawke's Bay
10. Marlborough
11. Chatham Islands
12. Westland County
13. New Munster
14. New Leinster
15. Westland Province
16. Canterbury

CHAPTER 4

CULTURE AND TRADITION

New Zealanders are warm, friendly, and hospitable people. We are easy to talk to and will not hesitate to reach out and say hello even to strangers.

Kiwis are highly sensitive to environmental concerns and work a lot to preserve and enhance their country's natural beauty. One of the strictest laws directly connected to the environment is that no natural products such as food, wood, cane, etc. are allowed to be imported into the country.

Even packaged foods that visitors bring into the country have to be declared at the customs and officials can inspect them at will. If you don't declare even those food items that are allowed to be brought into the country, then you can be fined heavily.

Also, please remember that you cannot bring in meat, fresh fruit and vegetables, fish, honey and other bee products into New Zealand

Greeting in New Zealand is very informal either with a handshake or a smile. The Maoris use hongi, pressing their noses together, as a form of greeting. We also have a casual approach and easily get into a first-name basis with everyone around.

Gift-giving is commonly practiced among Kiwis. If you are invited to someone's home, you must remember to carry a simple, valuable gift such as chocolates, flowers, or even a little book about your country.

Pop Quiz!

What is the name of a formal Maori welcome process?

1. Powhiri
2. Aotearoa
3. Iwi

(Answer — 1. Powhiri)

Dunedin Cadbury Chocolate Carnival

The reason I spoke about Baldwin Street is that an annual Cadbury Chocolate Carnival is held on this street every year. The start of this delightful festival is marked by rolling down giant Jaffa balls (read more on Jaffa balls under the 'Popular Foods' section).

This chocolate carnival also has numerous competitions, a Crunchie train, and a host of other chocolate-filled activities.

Pop Quiz!

The world's steepest street at an angle of 38 degrees is in New Zealand. Can you name the street?

1. Baldwin Street
2. Cook Street
3. Tasman Street

(Answer — 1. Baldwin Street located in Dunedin, a city in the South Island)

Important Maori Festivals

The Maoris still celebrate and follow age-old customs with fervor even today. Here are some of festivals, rituals, and traditions that have become very popular among all Kiwis and leave the visitors enthralled.

You are likely to come across this form of greeting frequently while traveling through North Island where most of the Maoris live.

Hongi – The Hongi is a traditional Maori greeting gesture that is done by touching your nose and forehead with that of the person you are greeting. Like a handshake but this gesture is more intimate and brings people closer to each other than a simple handshake or a smile.

Hongi is also referred to as the 'breath of life,' and legend states this tradition started when Hineahuone, the first Maori woman, was born. She was initially made of clay and was brought to life by a 'breath of life' given by the god Tane through her nostrils.

Haka – Haka is a Maori war dance that has been made very popular by New Zealand All Blacks, the national rugby team. Haka is an action-packed dance that includes the famous tongue-poking, powerful stomps of the feet, and widened eyes.

The Haka is used in several Maori ceremonies and also to welcome and honor special guests. You can witness this dance at Rotorua as it is used there to welcome visitors.

Ta Moko – Ta Moko are tattoos that men wear on their butts, thighs, and faces while women wear them on their chins and lips. The Maoris believe that the face is the most important and sacred part of the body making it a popular place for body tattoos. Many of the Maori locals wear their Ta Moko with pride.

Hangi – Don't confuse this with Hongi, which is a Maori form of formal greeting. Hangi is a cooking technique that has been in use for thousands of years. However, these days, the Hangi technique is used only for special occasions.

Meats, potatoes, and other vegetables are placed over hot stones in large pits dug in the ground. The food items are left to be cooked like this for three hours, then the entire community will have delicious food to eat.

Whakairo – Whakairo is an art of carving used by the Maoris to carry forward stories to the next generation. Whakairo is a form of expressing cultural histories and personal stories by the Maori people. There are special Whakairo artists who still carry on this traditional form of carving on various objects like building, canoes, weapons, and musical instruments.

Other Unique Facts about New Zealand

The longest name of any place in the world is Taumatawhakatangihangakoauauotamateapokaiwhenuakitanatahu, which is a hill in Hawkes Bay! Don't try to read it!

• New Zealand is the only country that has a National Wizard.

• Gisborne Airport, located on the east coast of North Island, has a railway track running in the middle of the runway. Many times, either the train or the plane has to stop to allow the other to move.

• The population of New Zealand is so small that there are more vending machines in Japan than they are people in my country.

Pop Quiz!

Can you guess the logo of the Royal New Zealand Air Force?

1. The kiwi
2. The parrot
3. The dolphin

(Answer — 1. The kiwi!)

Interesting Facts about the Lord of the Rings and its New Zealand Connection

Almost the entire shooting of the Lord of the Rings trilogy was shot in New Zealand. Here are some more interesting facts:

• The shooting of these films brought in NZD200 million into the country's economy.

• The country even has a Ministry for the Lord of the Rings to make sure all money due to us from the films is received.

• The currency notes of New Zealand have hobbit-related images.

National Holidays

New Zealanders celebrate the following national holidays with great pomp.

January 1 — New Year's Day
Nearly all New Year's Day celebrations take place out in the open with thousands of Kiwis participating.

A special place to be in on New Year's Day is Whangamata as more than 60,000 people gather here to take part in grand parties and celebrations.

Gisborne is another place where people flock during New Year to catch a glimpse of the first rays of the rising sun on New Year's Day.

New year, Fireworks Auckland City, New Zealand

Pop Quiz!

Do you know the actual birthday of the Queen of England?

1. April 21
2. December 25
3. June first week

(Answer - April 21st)

ANZAC DAY
Lest We Forget
····· 25 April ·····

April 25 — ANZAC Day

ANZAC Day is a day to remember the soldiers who lost their lives in all the wars fought on behalf of Australia and New Zealand.

January 2 — The Day after New Year This day is also a national holiday in my country. And yes, it is officially called the 'Day after New Year.'

February 6 — Waitangi Day
This day commemorates and remembers the signing of the Treaty of Waitangi in 1840 and was declared a national holiday in 1974.

The first Monday in June - Queen's birthday

In New Zealand, the Queen's birthday is celebrated on the first Monday of June to coincide with preceding and following holidays so that people get a nice, long break. Two important things happen on this day in New Zealand.

• The first important activity is the release of the Queen's Birthday Honor's List where people from different fields are honored for their work and for their contributions to the community and the country.

• The second important activity that usually takes place on this day is the opening of the ski season.

December 25 — Christmas Day

As New Zealand is located in the Southern Hemisphere, Christmas Day comes in the middle of summer. The festival is celebrated with a lot of pomp and show.

Local churches and business houses organize Santa parades in all neighborhoods. These parades happen any time from mid-November to Christmas, and the entire town participates.

Kids in New Zealand leave carrots for Santa's reindeer and pineapple chunks and even beer for Santa himself.
In big cities like Christchurch and Auckland, there are huge displays and splendid light shows.

We have our own special carols for Christmas like 'Christmas in New Zealand,' 'Te Haranui,' a Maori carol, and 'A Kiwiana Christmas.'

The fourth Monday in October — Labor Day

This important national holiday commemorates and remembers all the people who fought for an eight-hour working day. This amazing feat was achieved in New Zealand way back in 1840 when a carpenter named Samuel Parnell got to work for 8 hours a day for the first time in the world.

The first Labor Day in New Zealand was celebrated on 28 October 1890 to mark the 50th anniversary of this great man's achievement. And in 1899, a law was passed to make Labor Day a national holiday.

December 26 — Boxing Day
The day after Christmas is celebrated as Boxing Day in New Zealand.

Good Friday and Easter Monday- These holidays typically fall between late March and early April. Easter activities include a lot of socializing with friends and family, yearly vacations to exotic locations, family break-fasts and dinners, and making Easter eggs.

Other than these holidays, each of the 16 provinces has a Province Day celebrated on different dates each year.

New Zealand with its vast, long coastline is home to some delicious, fresh seafood. We love our seafood, and you should try a few dishes while traveling through my country.

Popular Foods

Roast lamb is another favorite food of the Kiwis. New Zealand lamb is one of our topmost export items and is popular all across the world. Kiwis make a yummy roast lamb dish adding a lot of seasonal vegetables (and definitely sweet potato or kumara) and with the flavor of rosemary.

Pork, chicken, and mutton cooked using the Maori Hangi cooking technique is another favorite meal for all Kiwis. In fact, visitors can indulge in an authentic Maori experience including a great feast cooked the hangi way in the town of Rotorua in the central part of North Island.

Other popular dishes you must try out during your visit are:

Jaffa

Jaffa are little orange-flavored, sugar-coated balls of chocolates that are a favorite with both adults and kids. Can you recall the name of the street on which giant Jaffa are rolled down to kickstart the annual chocolate carnival?

1. Baldwin Street in Dunedin
2. Cook Street
3. Tasman Street

(Answer — 1. Baldwin Street in Dunedin; the steepest road in the world)

Manuka honey

This special honey is made by the bees that pollinate the native bush called Manuka and has been used by the Maoris for hundreds of years to treat wounds and infections. In fact, the Maoris use the sap, bark, and leaves of the Manuka bush for medicinal purposes.

Today, Manuka honey is famous all over the world and is exported to international markets. You must remember to take some samples for your home.

Pavlova

The Aussies and Kiwis have a big argument about where this amazing food item was invented. The Aussies will say that Pavlova was invented in Australia and Kiwis will argue that it was invented in New Zealand. It really doesn't matter who wins this debate. What matters is that Pavlova is one of the most loved desserts in New Zealand, Australia, and all over the world. It is made with whipped cream, meringue, and served with seasonal fruits.

Fish-n-chips is British food influence that we Kiwis have taken into our lives. We love fish and chips, and the best way to eat them is to sit on a beach and munch on these goodies.

Whitebait fritters

Whitebait refers to immature fish that are not more than 1-2 inches in length. These little fish are caught fresh from the sea and converted into delicious fritters that everyone loves. The dish is highly popular in the West Coast of South Island.

Paua

Paua is the local name of a large sea snail. Paua is a favorite seafood in New Zealand and is eaten in a variety of ways like fritters, curries, and is also eaten raw. The paua shells are used to make jewelry and other decorative items.

Lemon & Paeroa

This lemony and sweet soft drink is totally Kiwi in origin. You can find it on the shelves of supermarkets alongside other global soft drinks brands.

Kumara

Kumara is Maori for sweet potato. Brought to New Zealand by the early Maori settlers, this food continues to be a favorite vegetable for the Kiwis. One of the best ways to eat kumara is by cooking it using the hangi technique. But, it can also be included in your meals in the usual cooking ways.

Animals Native to New Zealand

Kiwis - I think it makes sense to start this section with the most easily recognizable bird in New Zealand, the kiwi. Here are some fascinating facts about these amazing little birds:

- Kiwis are an endangered species of flightless birds that are native to New Zealand.

- Kiwis lay the largest egg in proportion to their size. A kiwi egg takes up nearly 20% of the mother's body!

- Since the eggs are big, there is a lot more yolk in them, which makes it possible for little kiwis to hatch out completely feathered, healthy, and ready to lead an independent life without help from parents.

- Kiwis have a highly developed 'nose,' which is a rare thing for birds. These are the only birds that have nostrils at the end of their beaks. Their sense of smell is so strong that they can smell food even under-ground.

Bats

Also referred to as pekapeka, bats are unique in New Zealand because they are the only land mammals native to the country. All other land mammals were imported. There are three species of bats in NZ including:

- The lesser and greater short-tailed bat - The short-tailed bat is an endangered species that is found only in certain areas of New Zealand.

- The long-tailed bat — This species is classified as 'nationally critical,' and all efforts are being made to preserve and enhance their numbers.

The Maoris associate bats with mythical nocturnal creatures called hokioi and believe that they foretell disaster and death.

Penguins — Found in the southeast parts of the country, the yellow-eyed penguins are one of the 6 species of penguins found here. You can also see this particular species on Stewart Island and the Banks Peninsula.

You can also catch different species of penguins at the Banks Peninsula, which houses the largest colony of little blue penguins and white-flippered little blue species.

In Oamaru, you can see both yellow-eyed and blue penguins just before sunset. You can also spot random penguins on the Otago Peninsula beaches and Marlborough Sounds.

Pop Quiz!

Which place is also called penguin town in New Zealand?

1. Banks Peninsula
2. Steward Island
3. Oamaru

(Answer — 3. Oamaru)

Kea - Kea is a native bird of New Zealand, which is known for a unique habit. It pulls off the windshield wipers from cars and eats up the rubber strips inside. Many car owners suffer damages because of this little, naughty, and cheeky parrot.

Hamilton's Frog — This species of frog is critically endangered and are found only on Stephen's Island, which lies on Cook Strait. These frogs is do not croak.

Hector's Dolphin — You can see the world's smallest species of dolphins riding the waves off the coast of South Island.

The Hooker's Sea Lion
You can find these most endangered sea lion species in the world relaxing on the beaches of Otago Peninsula and in the Catlins.

Tuatara — These animals are the only living reptile species from the age of the dinosaurs which is why tuataras are referred to as 'the living dinosaur.' An interesting feature about these reptiles is that they have a third eye on top of their heads!

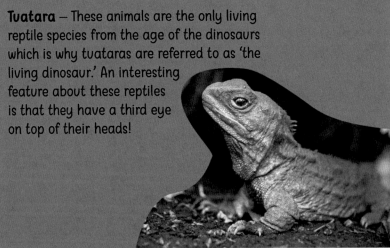

New Zealand fur seal — These creatures were once hunted for their meat. But, now they are a protected species and can be seen along the coastline of South Island.

Chevron Skink — These unique lizards are found only on the Little Barrier Island and the Great Barrier Island. They are the longest lizards in the country and are known to be very secretive.

Wood pigeon

Called kereru, the wood pigeon is native to New Zealand. The difference between these wood pigeons and the normal street pigeons is that the former have magnificently colored feathers. These birds, however, are horrible fliers, and many times, you can hear them landing awkwardly on the branches of trees.

Morepork – Also referred to as ruru, this bird is the only surviving native owl of New Zealand. They are stealthy predators, and you can hardly hear them as they swoop down on insects and other small animals. The Maoris believe that moreporks are guardian spirits.

New Zealand falcon – These birds of prey can be found only in New Zealand, and even here, they are not commonly sighted. You could catch sight of them at some bird sanctuaries.

Tui – With an unusual, almost robot-like call, tui are common birds found only in New Zealand. Their feathers are almost black with a few streaks of blue. They also sport two white feathers under their neck. Tui can be sighted in most native forest areas of the country.

Giant weta — This cockroach-like creature is the largest insect in the world that can grow to the size of a sparrow.

Kakapo — This very unusual flightless parrot is found only in New Zealand. It looks like an owl because of its prominent facial disc made of fine feathers, so it is also called owl parrot or even night parrot. Here are some really interesting facts about this native and unique parrot of New Zealand:

• It is the only parrot species in the world that cannot fly. These birds climb tall trees in the forest and then use their wings like a parachute to glide to the ground.

• They use their strong and powerful legs to get around.

• Their self-defense mechanism is to freeze in hopes of blending into the green environment. This method saves them from eagles but not land predators.

• As they are very friendly birds, the Maoris and Europeans used to keep kakapos as pets.

New Zealand fantail — This unique bird is one of the most well-known birds of New Zealand. They are found in abundance all over the country, and can even fly up to human beings. They are called piwakawaka in the Maori language. The reason for their name is because they have a fan-like tail.

The Legend of Pelorus Jack

At this point, it makes sense to tell you an interesting story about a legendary dolphin. During the late 19th and early 20th century, people believe a dolphin named Pelorus Jack guided ships through the French Pass, a highly dangerous, rocky channel that passes via the D'Urville Islands.

The French Pass had seen multiple shipwrecks caused by strong ocean currents and rocky waters. But, when Pelorus Jack was at work, no wrecks took place.

The friendly dolphin was first noticed by humans when he appeared in front of a ship from Boston called Brindle. When the ship was approaching the French Pass, the dolphin was sighted, and at first, the crew members wanted to kill him. However, the captain's wife was able to dissuade them from killing the poor creature.

After that, the dolphin went on to guide the ship through the treacherously narrow French Pass. Pelorus Jack guided numerous ships after this particular sighting.

Native Plants of New Zealand

Here are some of the plants and trees that are native to my beautiful country:

Kowharawhara — This tree has many species with the coastal ones sprouting silver-green leaves, and those that grow on rocks produce green flowers and purple fruit. The fruit of the Kowharawhara trees is eaten by the Maori people.

Kauri

The kauri is a majestic coniferous tree native to New Zealand. The tree can grow up to 60 meters (196 feet) in height and live up to 2000 years. However, today, trees that are more than 1700 years old are very rare.

The largest kauri tree, named Tane Mahuta, the Maori forest god, is in the Waipoua Forest in Northland Province. Nearly 3/4th of the kauri trees in New Zealand are in the Waipoua Forest.

Nikau — Nikau is a tall, beautiful palm tree that has a slender trunk and green fronds. You can find the nikau palm in lowland forests all over North Island and also in the northern parts of South Island. Nikau fronds are used by the Maori people to weave baskets and also to thatch the roofs of their huts.

Pohutukawa – Called as New Zealand's Christmas tree, it is one of the most iconic flowering trees of the country, growing along the coasts or hanging over cliffs all along North Island. The flowers are a bright, vibrant red and look like bottlebrushes. In December, the mature Pohutukawa trees burst into a crimson blaze.

Kowhai – Kowhai trees bloom in spring with golden yellow flowers that attract birds and insects. You can find them all over New Zealand both in the main islands as well as offshore islands.

Here are some more amazing facts about New Zealand's flora and fauna

South Island is home to a carnivorous snail that eats up worms like spaghetti.

New Zealand was home to the largest bird in the world called moa.

There are no snakes in my country at all. True/False? True, there are no snakes at all in New Zealand.

My country has a very high sheep-to-man ratio. The human population is around 4 million, and the sheep population is around 30 million.

Pop Quiz!

There are three kiwis in New Zealand; the people, the fruit, and the birds. What is the original name of the kiwi fruit?

1. New Zealand apples
2. Chinese gooseberries
3. It was always called the kiwi fruit

(Answer – 2. Chinese gooseberries)

FAMOUS PEOPLE FROM NEW ZEALAND

Even though my country is not very big and the population is small, many famous people who have made big contributions to the world are from here. Let me tell you about a few of them.

Edmund Hillary

The first human beings to reach the peak of Mount Everest were Edmund Hillary and his Sherpa companion, Tenzing Norgay. Edmund Hillary was born in Auckland on July 20, 1919. His height was 6 feet 5 inches.

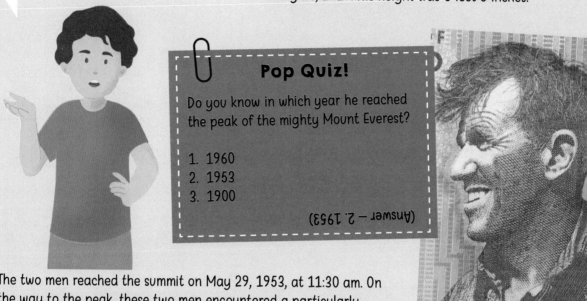

Pop Quiz!

Do you know in which year he reached the peak of the mighty Mount Everest?

1. 1960
2. 1953
3. 1900

(Answer — 2. 1953)

The two men reached the summit on May 29, 1953, at 11:30 am. On the way to the peak, these two men encountered a particularly difficult 40-ft rock face that Edmund Hillary found a way to climb over. This rock face is now called Hillary Step.

Hillary Trail Waitakere Ranges Auckland New Zealand

He also took an expedition to the South Pole. A Walking Trail called the Hillary Trail on the West Coast of Auckland is named in his honor. He was knighted for his contribution to mountaineering, and he became Sir Edmund Hillary. He later wrote many books about his climbing experiences including The Crossing of Antarctica, High Adventure, and No Latitude for Error.

Sir Peter Jackson

Famous for the Lord of the Rings trilogy, Peter Jackson was born on October 31, 1961, in Pukerua Bay in Porirua close to Wellington. The community of Pukerua Bay is very small with a population of just over 2000. When Peter Jackson was born, his small village had only 800 people living there.

Here are some amazing facts about this brilliant filmmaker:

When he was 17 years old, he applied for a job at Kiwi production company Film Unit. But, his job application was rejected. Later on, he bought that company.

As a teenager, he went on a long train journey to the north of New Zealand. The book he brought to pass the time during this long travel was Lord of the Rings. So, now you know when the spark to make the trilogy was lit up in his mind.

He is famous for coming to the film shoots in his shorts with bare feet. In an interview, he said that he wore shoes only on formal occasions. Going around barefoot is a common habit among the Kiwis who love to feel the grass under their feet. He was knighted in 2010.

Sir Ernest Rutherford

He won the Nobel Prize in Chemistry in 1908 before his most significant achievement- research work that led to the splitting of the atom to produce nuclear energy. Today, numerous streets, institutions, and buildings are named in his honor in New Zealand as well as in other parts of the world.

Pop Quiz!

What is Sir Ernest Rutherford popularly known as in the world of science?

1. The Father of Chemistry
2. The Father of Biology
3. The Father of Nuclear Physics

(Answer — 3. The Father of Nuclear Physics)

Sir Ernest Rutherford was born on 30 August 1871 in Brightwater, a small town about 12 miles southwest of Nelson. A memorial has been set up in his honor here that is open for visitors. Here are some interesting facts about this great scientist:

- An element called Rutherfordium is named after him.

- He first studied at Canterbury College before he moved to the University of Cambridge in 1895.

- He was knighted in 1914 for his contributions to science.

Russell Crowe

Russell Crowe is an easily recognizable person in movies. He was born on 7 April 1964 in Wellington. Before becoming a famous actor, Russell Crowe was a singer with the stage name of Russ Le Roq. He was also part of a rock band called 30 Odd Foot of Grunts.

He was offered a seat in National Institute for Dramatic Art, a prestigious institution of Australia. He worked very hard and took up a lot of roles and different kinds of jobs to make enough money to pay for his college fees.

During this time, he worked as a car washer, fruit picker, waiter, and hotel manager to earn as much money as he could. However, by 21 years of age, he became an established actor and decided not to take up the seat offered to him.

He loves horses as much as people. In an interview, he once said that he finds it difficult to say goodbye to his horse co-stars after the movie is completed.

Pop Quiz!

What is Russell Crowe's nickname?

1. Rusty
2. He does not have a nickname
3. Crowe

(Answer – 1. Rusty)

Pop Quiz!

What is the voice type in which Dame Kiri Te Kanawa sang?

1. Soprano
2. Tenor
3. Contralto

(Answer – 1. Soprano; it is the highest voice type for a female; a soprano is almost always the heroine in an opera.)

Dame Kiri Te Kanawa

The acclaimed Opera singer, Dame Kiri Te Kanawa is from New Zealand. She was born in Gisborne, a beautiful city on the east coast of North Island. Captain James Cook made his first landfall on the shores of this city.

Although she was a famous singer, what catapulted her to becoming a household name in the field of opera is when she sang at the wedding of Princess Diana and Prince Charles in 1981. Her brilliant performance was seen live by over 600 million people worldwide!

She was born Claire Mary Teresa Rawstron, but when Maori parents adopted her, her name changed to Kiri Te Kanawa.

Jane Campion

Elizabeth Jane Campion is one of the most well-known director-producers from New Zealand. She was born on 30 April 1954 in Wellington. Both her parents were from the world of art and theater. Her mother was an actress, and her father was a director of theater and opera.

She won an award for her first short film Peel at the 1986 Cannes Film Festival, which brought her recognition and fame. Her first TV film was Two Friends made in 1986, and her first film was Sweetie in 1989.

She has gone to win many awards including the coveted Oscar for Best Screenplay Writing in 1994 for a movie called The Piano. She was knighted in 2016 for her immense contribution to films.

Pop Quiz!

What title do women get when they are knighted?

1. Sir; same as men
2. Madam
3. Dame

(Answer — 3. Dame)

Steven Adams

Steven Adams is an NBA superstar from New Zealand. He was born on 20 July 1993 in Rotorua in central North Island. Rotorua is one of the top tourist hotspots in the country.

He identifies himself strongly with Maori culture. He says the reason he chooses to play for the Oklahoma City Thunder is that Oklahoma reminds him of his home country, New Zealand.

He started playing for the Oklahoma City Thunder in 2013 and continues with them today. Steven Adams was named as one of the top 100 highest-paid athletes in 2018.

He loves comics and Japanese anime. In fact, for his 25th birthday, he released a comic called Kiwi Legend based on his own life.

His sister, Valerie Adams, has won the shot put gold multiple times in the Olympic Games.

Lorde

Lorde is a new-age singing star from New Zealand. She achieved world-fame with her debut singles album Royals. Lorde was born in a small, quaint village called Takapuna in Auckland. She spent her childhood in Davenport, a small suburb in Auckland. Here are some interesting facts about this famous person:

Her real name is Ella Marija Lani Yelich-O'Connor. She took on the stage name of Lorde after the success of her Royals album, which also reflects her obsession about everything old and royal.

She has a strange and rare neurological condition called synesthesia, which is good for her profession because it allows her to see colors when musical notes are played. She combines these colors and the music to create harmony and hit songs.

Neil Finn

Neil Finn was born on 27 May 1958 in Te Awamutu, a small town in Waikato in North Island. Crowded House has sold more than 10 million albums across the world. He is considered to be New Zealand's equivalent of John Lennon. Some of his top songs are:

- "Don't Dream Its Over"
- "Mean To Me"
- "Something So Strong"
- "Into Temptation"

Pop Quiz!

What is the name of the rock band founded by Neil Finn?

1. Crowded House
2. House of Two
3. The Rock Band of New Zealand

(Answer — 1. Crowded House)

MAJOR CITIES AND ATTRACTIONS

In addition to stunning natural vistas of lakes, rivers, and mountains, New Zealand is home to multiple modern and highly urbanized cities as well. Let me tell you about a few of my favorite cities around the country.

Auckland

Auckland is the largest city in New Zealand in terms of population (about 1.5 million) and size. In fact, the population of this beautiful city is larger than the entire region of South Island.

Visitors have a variety of hotspots to see and experience. You can visit parks attached to native bushes, numerous golden sandy beaches, gorgeous islands just off the coast in Hauraki Gulf, and all this with the conveniences and luxuries of a well-developed city.

The city itself is easily comparable to the best, modern cities of the world with numerous options to shop, eat, and stay. The amazing nightlife and the food scene are some of the top attractions for most visitors to Auckland. Here are some of the top things you must not miss while in Auckland:

Sky Tower

Sky Tower — With a revolving restaurant perched right on top of this stunning, manmade structure, the Sky Tower is a must-see in Auckland. The observation tower gives you a 360-degree view of the marvelous city and its skyscrapers.

Here are some surprising facts about the Sky Tower in Auckland:

It is 1076 feet high, making it the tallest manmade building in the Southern Hemisphere.

It has three observation decks, and all of them offer a stunning 360-degree view of the city.

Three elevators can take up 225 people every 15 minutes. So, you never have to wait for very long to reach the top.

Pop Quiz!

Can you guess how long the elevator ride to the top takes?

1. 5 minutes
2. 3 minutes
3. 40 seconds

(Answer — 3. 40 seconds; the elevator travels at a speed of 18 kmph or about 11 mph)

Waihek

A trip to this wonderful island is a great way to spend a day. A 40-minute ferry ride from Auckland gets you to Waiheke. You can see beautiful beaches and vineyards. This island is best visited during the summer season.

Vineyard on the green hillside - Waiheke Island

Wellington

Beehive, the Executive Wing of the New Zealand Parliament Buildings in Wellington City

With a population of about 500,000, Wellington is the capital of New Zealand. This wonderful city, which is my home too, is surrounded by beautiful vineyards, mountains, and coastlines. Wellington is often referred to as one of the 'coolest' cities in the world.

Another beautiful waterfront city like Auckland, Wellington has a lot to offer for visitors ranging from beaches, museums, and botanical gardens.

Pop Quiz!

What is the name of the Parliament Building in Wellington?

1. The Den
2. The House
3. The Beehive

(Answer – 3. The Beehive)

Here are some interesting facts about the capital city of New Zealand:

• It is the southernmost capital city in the world.

• Some of the steepest streets are found in Wellington. Many of Wellingtonians walk to their workplaces, and therefore, are quite fit compared to other city dwellers.

• Wellington replaced Auckland as the capital of New Zealand in 1865.

Botanic Gardens – The Botanic Gardens in Wellington is spread over 26 hectares (64 acres) that offer beautiful, unique land-scapes, gorgeous floral displays, wonderful sculptures, and exotic native forest areas.

Lambton Quay – Wellington is home to a vast multitude of restaurants and cafes. The number of cafes/restaurants per person in Wellington is more than in New York. Lambton Quay is the heart of Wellington and a must-visit to get a view of fantastic shopping areas, cafes, hotels, and restaurants.

Some places that you must see while in Wellington:

Christchurch

Christchurch Tramway, classic transportation in New Zealand

With a population of just about 360,000, Christchurch is a city for surfing, beautiful parks and gardens, artworks, and a place that backpackers love. Experts believe that Christchurch was one of the first places inhabited by the early Polynesian settlers who hunted moa birds.

Christchurch began its journey to modernity when European whalers and sealers landed here in 1840. In 1848, numerous British pilgrims landed here and wanted to build a city around a college and cathedral, like in Christ Church, Oxford. So, the name Christchurch was given to the place in 1848.

During spring and autumn, Christchurch is especially breathtaking to look at as all the trees in its numerous parks and gardens bloom and blossom in all their colorful splendor. Here are some places to visit in Christchurch:

International Antarctic Center – This amazing place has been created so that visitors can experience Antarctica in Christchurch. You can experience Antarctica Storms, enjoy the spectacle and thrill of Antarctica Snow and Ice, slide down icy slides, and ice caves.
Also, visit the Antigua Boatsheds, take a boat cruise down River Avon, and don't miss the bustling area that has been rehabilitated after the 2011 earthquake that devastated the region.

Hamilton

Hamilton, also referred to as the Tron, is located on the banks of the majestic Waikato River. Hamilton is situated right in the middle of the Waikato region. Hamilton is used as a center to visit other towns close by such as Waitomo, Raglan, and even Rotorua. Some of the top places you must visit in Hamilton are:

Hamilton Gardens These stunning gardens are one of the biggest draws in Hamilton. You can use guided tours or take a walk by yourself through various theme gardens like the Italian Renaissance Garden, Chinese Scholars' Garden, Modernist Garden, Sustainable Backyard, Kitchen Garden, etc.

Waitomo Caves – Just a short drive from Hamilton will bring you to Waitomo Caves, which is home to millions of tiny glowworms. It is a sight to behold and worth taking a trip to this place.

Tauranga

This coastal city is close to many popular beaches with the backdrop of the amazing peak of Mount Maunganui. Tauranga translates to 'safe anchorage' referring to the place as the landing site of early settlers from Polynesia.

Most of the kiwi fruit production happens around the city of Tauranga, which is also known for excellent quality avocados and tangelos. The only saltwater lakes of New Zealand are found at the base of Mount Maunganui. Captain James Cook gave the name of Bay of Plenty to the regions in and around Tauranga because he noticed that all the Maori villages then had beautiful, well-maintained gardens.

The top attractions in Tauranga are:

Waimarino Adventure Park
This park is one of the best water parks in the country and has activities and rides for people of all ages including big and small kids.

Mount Maunganui Walks
You can take a walk up this iconic mountain, and if you can do it early in the morning, then you can catch a glimpse of one of the best sunrise vistas in the world from here.

Napier

Napier is best loved by artists as you will get to see numerous beautifully and artistically restored old buildings. In 1931, a tremendous earthquake lasting three minutes completely destroyed the central business district of Napier. A lot of reconstruction and rebuilding took place immediately after that devastating earthquake resulting in a beautiful, artistic city.

The Sea Walls Collection is a set of 50 walls spread across the city which are painted with beautiful murals. Napier is best known for its art deco architecture.

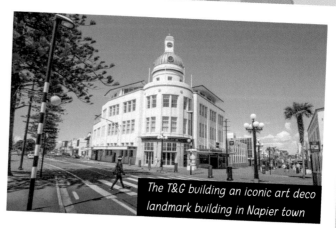

The T&G building an iconic art deco landmark building in Napier town

The best way to enjoy Napier is to go on self-guided walks. Other activities that you will love here are visits to beautiful vineyards, excellent cafes and bars, and restaurants.

Dunedin

Known as the student city of New Zealand, Dunedin has much to offer visitors and tourists too. Here are some amazing facts about this underrated city:

University of Otago - Dunedin, New Zealand

Amazing beaches — Some of the best beaches in the country are located in Dunedin. The coastline of Dunedin is quite wild and untamed but beautiful to surf, sail, kayak, and row.

The Otago Farmer Markets — These markets offer the best and the freshest produce all year round. The vendors are all locals who find the best fruit and vegetables for you. Don't miss out visiting this fun place. There are numerous eateries where you will get your favorite New Zealand dishes.

The Otago Settlers Museum and Otago Museum — These museums celebrate the rich history and culture of Dunedin and students from the different colleges in the city have added interesting, modern tidbits to these museums.

Nelson

Aerial view from the center of New Zealand, Nelson

With many national parks at driving distances from Nelson and the weather being what it is in the city, this place is the perfect spot for all your wilderness trips in New Zealand. Facing the Tasman Sea, there are numerous, stunning beaches too.

Another unique thing about Nelson is that it is the only large city of New Zealand that does not have a railway connection.

Blue Lake, New Zealand, Lake, South Island

The national parks that you must visit while in Nelson are:

Mount Olympus - Kahurangi National Park

Kahurangi National Park – This beautiful park reserve is diverse, wild, and is home to marble mountains and some stunning beaches. You will see rare plants and animals, strange plants, and ancient rocks within the confines of this park.

Abel Tasman National Park – This wilderness reserve is famous for a long walking trail along the coast called Abel Tasman Coast Track.

Nelson Lakes National Park
You can try a lot of outdoor activities here ranging from easy-to-do walking tracks along the lakes to really challenging mountain hikes. Right at the center of this huge national park (over 100,000 hectares or 247,000 acres) are two beautiful, alpine lakes namely Rotoroa and Rotoiti.

As per Maori legend, these two lakes were created by the great chief, Rakaihaitu, when he was digging holes with his digging stick, or ko. One of the holes became Lake Rotoroa, which means 'large waters,' and a second hole became Lake Rotoiti or 'small waters.'
Other important cities and towns in New Zealand are Gisborne, the place where the first sunrise is seen, the gorgeous Queenstown, and Rotorua, where you can experience Maori culture.

CONCLUSION

That brings us to the end of our New Zealand trip. I hope you enjoyed it as much as I enjoyed taking you around my wonderful country. I would like to end the trip with a little fun quiz on New Zealand. But, before that, can you tell me about your experience?

Which was your most favorite place in New Zealand? Why did you like this place so much?

What was your favorite dish? Would you try making it in your house and let your friends taste it?

If you had a chance to visit my country again, which is the place you will definitely not missing visiting? Why?

Now, on to the quiz:

What is the name of the traditional form of cooking used by Maoris that is still popular?

1. Hongi
2. Hangi
3. Grilling

Can you name the cheeky parrot that eats the rubber from car windscreen wipers?

1. Kakapo
2. Kiwi
3. Kea

(Answer — 2. Hangi)

(Answer — 3. Kea)

What is the name of the city in New Zealand that sees sunrise first every day?

1. Hamilton
2. Gisborne
3. Nelson

(Answer – 2. Gisborne)

Which city in New Zealand has the highest population?

1. Wellington
2. Auckland
3. Hamilton

(Answer – 2. Auckland)

Which water body separates Australia and New Zealand?

1. The Cook Strait
2. The Tasman Sea
3. The Pacific Ocean

(Answer – 1. The Tasman Sea)

Name the famous treaty signed between Maori chiefs and the British Crown for which New Zealanders get a national holiday even today?

1. The Treaty of Waitangi
2. The Treaty of Waitomo
3. The Treaty of Aotearoa

(Answer – 1. The Treaty of Waitangi)

What is another name of Mount Cook?

1. Aoraki
2. Aotearoa
3. It does not have another name

(Answer – 1. Aoraki)

What was the old capital of New Zealand before Wellington?

1. Auckland
2. Hamilton
3. Nelson

(Answer – 1. Auckland)

What is the name of the caves in which glowworms are found in plenty?

1. Waitomo Caves
2. Strait Caves
3. Tasman Caves

(Answer – 1. Waitomo Caves)

So, that's all I have for now. How many were you able to answer without peeking? Do visit my country again, and I will tell you more about it.

Made in the USA
Monee, IL
22 August 2020